PURIT

PURITY
OF HEART

by

William Booth

Salvation Books
The Salvation Army International Headquarters
London, United Kingdom

First published 1902

Revised edition 2007
Reprinted 2010

Copyright © 2007
The General of The Salvation Army

ISBN 978-0-85412-766-5

Cover design by Nathan Sigauke

Published by Salvation Books
The Salvation Army International Headquarters
101 Queen Victoria Street, London EC4V 4EH
United Kingdom

Printed by UK Territory Print & Design Unit

CONTENTS

SERIES INTRODUCTION
'CLASSIC SALVATIONIST TEXTS'

This series is intended to help a new generation of readers become familiar with works published across the years by The Salvation Army and which over time have come to be regarded as 'classics' in Salvationist circles and even beyond.

It is hoped also that these republications might lead to a rediscovery of them and the truths they convey by those who once read them. They live on not only for their content, but also for the passionate spirit that breathes through what is written.

Salvationists have no desire to live in the past, but we are ready to recognise the debt we owe to those who have gone before. We look to the future, under God, taking with us the sacred heritage he has given. These writings are part of that heritage.

I hope and pray that this series will help and inspire all who use it, and that some will be prompted to contribute in written form to modern Salvationist literature in an age that needs also the old, eternal truths expressed in language for the 21st century.

The series is dedicated to the glory of God.

Shaw Clifton
General
London, July 2007

FOREWORD

How right it is to launch the 'Classic Salvationist Texts' series with a famous work by the Founder of The Salvation Army, William Booth. Some may have surpassed him in eloquence, others may have exceeded his intellectual appeal, but few have been his equal in writing for a verdict in the heart of the reader. He wrote to change lives.

Purity of Heart began as a series of letters to be read in weekly gatherings of the early Salvationists. The year was 1900. They ran for two whole years, entitled 'Letters from the General to the Soldiers of The Salvation Army'. The letters were read aloud in meetings held on Tuesday evenings across the United Kingdom, and often read again on the following Sunday morning. Similar steps were taken in every country where the Army was then serving and witnessing.

A selection of the letters was then released in book form by the Army in 1902.

The teaching of the blessing of a clean heart was and is a central tenet of Salvationism, reflecting our Wesleyan Methodist roots. Salvationists still seek it, claim it and testify about it, but far less than once they did. The Holy Spirit still waits graciously to grant it to all who seek in sincere faith. May the republishing of Booth's letters help to that end.

Shaw Clifton
General
London, July 2007

PREFACE

The following letters were, in the first instance, addressed to weekly meetings of salvation soldiers. They called forth so many expressions of thankfulness, and so many requests that they might be printed in permanent form, that I have gathered them together in this little book. They do not, of course, profess to treat this great subject with anything like completeness, nor do I make any claim for them to literary elegance of power; and yet, if they are used at all, they must go as they are, for I have no opportunity to properly revise them.

William Booth
General
London, January 1902

One

Purity – What is it?

My Dear Comrades,

We Salvationists are always singing or praying or talking about a pure heart. Indeed, there are few subjects of which we more frequently speak, or in which we more truly glory. Some of our most beautiful and heart-stirring songs are on this theme. Perhaps, no one is more frequently sung by us than that commencing:

> *O for a heart to praise my God,*
> *A heart from sin set free!*
> *A heart that always feels the Blood,*
> *So freely spilt for me!*

Is not that beautiful? But it goes on better still:

> *A heart in every thought renewed,*
> *And full of love divine;*
> *Perfect and right, and pure and good,*
> *A copy, Lord, of thine!*

Great, however, as is the power of such songs to stir our hearts, perhaps nothing delights the genuine Salvationist more than the definite testimonies of those living in the enjoyment of the blessing, or the earnest prayers for its bestowment, or the fervent appeals to comrades to secure this pearl of great price, so often heard of in our ranks.

And yet I am afraid that many of our soldiers do not definitely experience and openly profess the enjoyment of the blessing; and I have been thinking that, perhaps, it is because the subject is not so well understood as it should be. I propose, therefore, to try to explain it in a few letters, which I hope my comrades will carefully consider.

Now, please remember that my subject is 'Purity of Heart'. I want to explain what we mean by a pure heart; to show how you may obtain the precious treasure, if you are not possessed of it already; and how you may keep the blessing when attained.

I will start off by saying we all know what is meant by being pure. When we talk about the purity of things around us, we mean that they are clean and unadulterated. That is, that they are not only without dirt or filthiness, but have no inferior substance mixed with them.

When we say that a man is pure, in the religious sense, we mean that he is right and honest and true inside and out; that he not only professes, but practices the things that have to do with his duty to God and man. Sin is spoken of in the Bible as filthiness or defilement of the body, mind, or spirit. Purity in religion must mean, therefore, the absence of such filthy things as drunkenness, gluttony, dishonesty, cheating, falsehood, pride, malice, bad tempers, selfishness, unbelief, disobedience, or the like.

In short, to be pure in soul signifies deliverance from all and everything which the Lord shows you to be opposed to his holy will. It means that you not only possess the ability to live the kind of life that he desires, but that you actually do live it.

Now, purity, I need not tell you, my comrades, is much admired and greatly desired by all right-minded beings. To begin with: we all like material purity; for instance, I am sure that everyone reading this letter prefers to have a clean body. When you rise in the morning, you are not comfortable till you have washed yourselves. When the miners come from the pit, or the farmers from the field, or the girls from the factory, their first demand is for water with which to cleanse themselves.

You like clean clothes and clean linen, do you not? Consider the money and labour that are expended in keeping your garments clean. You like a clean home. See how the housewife scrubs and washes and brushes and dusts to keep the floor and windows and furniture clean. You like a clean city. What a laborious and costly sweeping of the streets, and carrying away of rubbish there is; and what money is spent on the fixing and cleansing of sewers to keep our towns and cities sweet and pure.

We like this sort of purity, because it is pleasant to the eye and good for health. We know that dirt is hateful to the senses, breeds vermin, generates cholera, plague and diseases in general, and hurries people to the grave. So we hate it, and say, 'Away with it; let us be clean!' But all right-minded beings admire the purity of the soul far more than they do the purity of the body, or the clothes, the home, or anything else; and that, because it is so much more important.

For instance:

(a) God loves soul purity. It is his nature to do so. I have no doubt, like us he prefers to see his children outwardly clean. He tells us, through Paul, that we are to have our bodies washed with pure water; but the washing of the heart is far more desirable to him than that of the body.

> *His saints are lovely in his sight,*
> *He views his children with delight;*
> *He sees their hope; he knows their fear,*
> *And looks, and loves his image there.*

Yes, God delights in holiness. Heaven, his dwelling-place, is pure. Its inhabitants are pure. Its employments, and enjoyments, and worship are all alike pure.

(b) The angels love purity. If any unholy creature could, by any means, be introduced into the Celestial City, the inhabitants would, I am sure, avoid such a creature, as we should avoid a being who had some dreadful disease.

(c) The devils know that purity is a precious thing, although they hate it and oppose it with all their might.

(d) Many wicked men admire purity. They look on it as being beautiful and desirable in others, although they regard it as being impossible to them. In their thoughtful moments, when the Spirit of God strives with them, when the recollections of the innocent days gone by crowd into their memories, and they see people who they know are clean and good, they hate themselves because of their own impurity, although all the time refusing to submit to God, and to accept the salvation that would make them pure.

(e) Lost souls in hell feel how infinitely superior holiness is to wickedness. They see now how much better it would have been for them if they had washed their hearts in the Blood of the Lamb when they had the privilege of doing so. Oh, what would they not give to have such opportunities as those enjoyed by you!

Are you in love with purity, my comrades? Perhaps you possess it. Perhaps you have been to Jesus for the cleansing power, laid yourselves at his feet, given up your doubtful things, offered yourselves to do his will, living or dying, and believed that the Blood of Jesus Christ has made you clean. Oh, if that experience has been yours, happy are you, and happier still if you are walking in the power and peace of that experience today. If it is so, I congratulate you; I delight in you and praise God on your account. But if this blessing is not yours, are you longing after it? Does the thought of it fill your soul with desire? Does it make you feel like the poet, when he sang:

> *O glorious hope of perfect love!*
> *It lifts me up to things above,*
> *It bears on eagles' wings;*
> *It gives my ravished soul a taste,*
> *And makes me for some moments feast*
> *With Jesus' priests and kings.*

Come along, my comrades. Your happiness and your influence are all connected with your being made holy. Oh, I beseech you to kneel down here and now, and ask God to make you each and all pure, by the power of the Holy Ghost, through the Blood of the Lamb.

Yours affectionately,
WILLIAM BOOTH

Two

Purity Commanded

My Dear Comrades,

I want again to take up the subject on which I wrote in my last letter. It is, indeed, a precious topic. I have loved it and talked about it all the way through my religious life; and, today, I regard the enjoyment and publication of the blessing of a clean heart as being as essential to my own peace, power and usefulness, and as necessary to the progress and prosperity of the Army as ever it was.

Let me proceed, then, with the work of explanation. A right understanding of the subject will help you to obtain this blessing for yourselves, and enable you to explain it to others.

In my last letter I talked about purity in general; in this I want to say something on the subject in its practical application to yourselves. What did our dear Lord mean when he spoke of the 'pure in heart' and pronounced them blessed? What is it to have a pure heart? To answer that question, I must begin by asking another: what is meant by the heart?

To which question I answer, we do not mean that organ which you can feel beating in your breast, and which is the central force of the bodily system. That is a very important part of man, and the keeping of it in good condition is most essential.

But it is not the heart in your body to which Jesus Christ referred in this passage, and about which I want to talk to you; but that power which, being the central force of your soul, may be said to answer to it. As the heart which palpitates in your bosom is the great driving-force of the natural man, so the heart we are talking about is the great driving force of the spiritual man.

(a) In this sense it is your heart that feels joy or sorrow. When you say, 'That poor woman died of a broken heart on account of the ill-treatment of her husband' you mean that it was the bitter anguish of her soul which killed her.

(b) It is the heart that chooses between right and wrong. When you say, 'My brother's heart is on the side of God, and goodness, and truth' you mean that these things are the supreme choice of his soul.

(c) It is the heart that decides on the particular line of conduct to be pursued. When you say, 'This young man went to the mercy seat and gave his heart to God' you mean that he decided, in his inmost soul, to accept salvation and become a soldier of Christ.

(d) It is the heart that loves righteousness and hates iniquity. When God says, 'My son, give me thy heart' he means, 'Come along, young man or woman, and love me and holiness, and souls, and hate the devil and sin, with all the powers you possess.'

(e) It is the heart that moulds the character, guides the choice, and masters all the course and conduct of a man's life. The heart is the captain of the ship. It determines whether a man shall accept mercy, serve God, follow righteousness, live for the salvation of his fellows, and finally enter the Heavenly Harbour in triumph, or whether he shall live a life of rebellion, die in his sins and finish up a wreck on the rocks of everlasting despair. How important it is to each one of us that we should have a good – a right – a pure heart.

Now, seeing that the heart is so thoroughly the master of the man, nothing can be much plainer, can it, my comrades, than the necessity for the heart being pure? But what is a pure heart? What is it to have a heart that has been cleansed by the power of the Holy Spirit through the Blood of Jesus Christ? That is a very important inquiry, and I do hope that my dear soldiers will give me their careful attention while I strive to answer it.

1. First, a pure heart is not a heart that is never tempted to do evil. Possibly there is no such thing in this world, nor ever has been, as a non-tempted heart, that is a man or a woman who has never been exposed to temptation to commit sin, of one kind or the other. Not only was our Blessed Lord tempted by the devil in the wilderness, but he was beset with evil attractions all the way through his life. The Apostle Paul expressly tells us that our Saviour was in all points tempted like as we are, but

hallelujah! he effectually resisted the world, the flesh and the devil, and came through the trying ordeal without a stain. He triumphed over all, for the apostle exultingly assures us that, 'He was without sin.'

You will be tempted, my comrades, all through your earthly journey, even to the very gates of Heaven; but, thank God, temptation is not sin, and grace, abundant grace, is provided to enable you to triumph over all the fascinations of earth and all the devices of hell. You can come off more than conqueror. But, remember, although you may have a pure heart you will have to fight temptation.

2. A pure heart is not a heart that cannot suffer. Beyond question, Jesus Christ had a pure heart; he was holy and undefiled, and yet he was 'The Man of Sorrows'. Paul tells us that although he exercised himself to have always a conscience void of offence towards God and towards man, yet was he not saved from being, at times, 'in heaviness through manifold temptations'.

3. By a pure heart we do not mean a heart that cannot sin. The devil was once a beautiful, sinless creature. But he yielded to temptation. The sinless crown fell from his beautiful brow, and from a pure archangel he was changed into a foul fiend, and hurled all the way from his bright and sinless Heaven to his dark and gloomy hell. Adam was pure when he came from the hands of his Maker. God pronounced him to be good; but, led away by

Satan, he lost his purity, and was cast out of Eden into a world of sin and sorrow and death.

Alas! Alas! We have the unspeakable sorrow of too frequently seeing saints and soldiers fall from holiness into sin. Some of the many miserable backsliders around us once walked closely with God, kept their garments unspotted from the world and were examples of all that is pure and good. But they have gone back to the beggarly elements of the world, and, like the sow that was washed, they are again wallowing in the mire.

So, my comrades, you will see that no matter however pure you may become, it will be possible for you to sin. Though you wash your garments white, and for a season walk with God in holy communion, and have faith so that you can remove mountains and save multitudes, you must remember that while you are in this life it is possible for you to fall from grace. Nay, you must remember that unless you take heed to yourselves, and watch and pray, the probabilities are that you will be overtaken by some besetting sin, and, after having saved others, become yourself a castaway. Therefore, 'let him that thinketh he standeth take heed lest he fall'.

4. By a pure heart, we do not mean any experience of purity, however blessed it may be, that cannot increase in enjoyment, usefulness and power. Pull the weeds out of your garden, and the flowers and plants and trees will grow faster, flourish more abundantly, and become more fruitful.

Just so, this very moment, let Jesus Christ purge the garden of your souls of envy and pride, and remove the poisonous plants of malice and selfishness and every other evil thing, and faith and peace, and hope and love, and humility and courage, and all the other beautiful flowers of Paradise will flourish in more charming beauty and more abundant fruitfulness.

Oh, will you not go down now before God and give yourselves fully over into the hands of your precious Saviour? He is waiting to sanctify you. Cast overboard all that hinders. It is God that purifies the heart. Will you let him do the work? Now cry out in faith:

> *Anger and sloth, desire and pride,*
> *This moment be subdued;*
> *Be cast into the crimson tide*
> *Of my Redeemer's Blood.*

But you must go a little further, my comrades, and boldly and believingly sing that song of triumph:

> *'Tis done, thou dost this moment save,*
> *With full salvation bless;*
> *Redemption through thy Blood I have,*
> *And spotless love and peace.*

Yours affectionately,
WILLIAM BOOTH

Three

Purity Means Deliverance

'That he would grant unto us, that we ... might serve him without fear, in holiness and righteousness before him, all the days of our life' (Luke 1:74, 75).

My Dear Comrades,

I hope that I shall not weary you by returning again to the question of a pure heart. The subject is so important to the whole Christian Church, to the entire Salvation Army, nay, to the wide, wide world, that it must be lifted up. Holiness has been so great a blessing to us in the past, and will, I am sure, be so much greater a blessing to us in the future, that I feel that it must be brought to the front. You must see its value, and understand its meaning. If you are not living in the enjoyment of the peace, power, and gladness of holiness, it is, possibly, because you entertain some mistaken notions respecting it. The ability of the devil to lead people astray on this, as on many other questions, is largely in proportion to his power to deceive them. Can I better make you understand what is meant by purity of heart?

You will remember that in my last letter I tried to show you that by a pure heart we did not mean a heart that could not, or would not, be tempted, or that could not, or would not, be called to suffer; nor that the soldier out of whose heart all impurity had been expelled could not sin, or would have reached such a state of experience beyond which he would not be able to grow in faith, and hope, and charity, and in all the graces of the Holy Spirit.

What, then, is a pure heart? I reply that a pure heart is a heart that has been cleansed by the Holy Spirit from all sin, and enabled to please God in all it does; to love him with all its powers, and its neighbour as itself. Where this experience is enjoyed by anyone it may be said that God has made the heart pure, even as he is pure.

But here I may be asked the question, 'Does not God bestow this wonderful deliverance from sin on the soul at conversion? Does he not sanctify and make it good and holy at the same time that he pardons its sins?' No, I reply; although a great work is done for the soul at conversion, its deliverance from sin at that time is not complete. It is true that he does a great deal for a man when he makes that remarkable change. He destroys the bondage in which sin holds the transgressor; but the destruction of sin out of the heart and out of the life is not entire. Here let me try and show you the difference in the purification that comes to a man when he is fully cleansed. I will do this by setting forth the three different states into which the soul can come with respect to sin:

1. Before a man or a woman is converted, some particular sin is the master of the soul. That is, some unlawful appetite or selfish passion always rules the individual, and makes him act as it dictates.

What do I mean by sin being the master? I answer that the unconverted soul is held by it in a bondage from which it cannot get away. It has no choice. It is under its power. It must sin. The soul may have light to see its evil and ruinous character. It may hate it, struggle against it, make resolutions never to do it again. But it is driven by its own nature to do the things that it does not want to do; and is prevented from doing the things that it wishes to do, often, as the Apostle Paul describes, crying out in bitterness of spirit as it struggles and fights with it, 'O wretched man that I am! Who shall deliver me from this wretched condition of slavery that is worse than death?'

This is the experience of every unsaved man and woman; at least of everyone who has light to see what an evil thing sin is. It is true that the character of the mastering sin will differ in different persons. In some people the governing evil may be something that is looked upon by the world as vulgar, such as drunkenness, or lust, or dishonesty, or gambling, or some other evil passion that has got hold of the sinner, and from which he cannot get away, and for which every precious thing on earth and in Heaven is sacrificed. In other cases it may be some sin that is not so much despised by what is called the respectable part of the community, such as pride, ambition, selfishness, secret infidelity or the like. But, in some form or other, sin rules in the heart of every ungodly man. He is mastered by sin.

2. Now, let us look at the second state into which a man can come with respect to sin. When he is saved, not only does he receive the pardon of sin, but deliverance from its bondage.

The yoke is broken, the fetters are snapped, the prison doors are opened, he is free! Instead of sin being his master, he is the master of sin. Instead of drink, or temper, or money-worship, or worldly pleasure, or some other devilish thing driving him down the broad way to destruction, against his judgment, against his own wishes, against the strivings of the Spirit, he is made free to do the will of God and to climb the narrow way to Heaven.

But, great and glorious as is the change wrought in the heart at conversion, maybe deliverance is not complete. The power of sin is broken, but there are still certain evil tendencies left in the soul. There are what the apostle terms 'the roots of bitterness'. These evils ordinarily grow and increase in power, involving the soul in constant conflict, and as the time goes by often gain the mastery, and as the result there is much sinning and repenting.

3. Then comes the third state. Tired of this conflict, hating these internal evils, weeping over the pride and malice, and envy and selfishness, that the soul still finds within, it rises up, and cries out:

Tell me what to do to be pure,
In the sight of the all-seeing eyes.
Tell me, is there no thorough cure,
No escape from the sins I despise?
Tell me, can I never be free
From this terrible bondage within?
Is there no deliverance for me?
Must I always have sin dwell within?

To this question God sends the glad answer back: 'Then will I sprinkle clean water upon you, and ye shall be clean: from all your filthiness, and from all your idols, will I cleanse you. A new heart also will I give you and a new spirit will I put within you; and I will take away the stony heart out of your flesh, and I will give you an heart of flesh. And I will put my Spirit within you, and cause you to walk in my statutes, and you shall keep my judgments, and do them.'

'All things are possible to him that believeth.' Then the soul believes, the sanctifying Spirit falls and the third stage is reached, which is salvation from all sin.

In the first stage the soul is under sin.

In the second stage the soul is over sin.

In the third state the soul is without sin.

In which stage are you, my comrades? Settle it for yourselves. Have you got a pure heart? Examine yourselves. What is your reply?

Some of you in describing your experience can adopt the words of the apostle, with a little variation, and say: the very God of peace has sanctified me wholly; and he preserves my whole spirit and soul and body blameless, and he will continue to do so unto the coming of our Lord Jesus Christ. Faithful is he that has called me to this experience of purity, who also will do it.

All glory to God, my comrades. Give him all the praise. Be careful to 'Walk in the light, as he is in the light', then shall you have fellowship with him and with other sanctified souls, and the Blood of Jesus Christ his Son shall keep you cleansed from all sin. In which case he will use you to promote his glory, make you useful, and show you still greater things.

To those who know that they do not possess a pure heart, I put the question, will you have one now?

God is waiting to cleanse you. What doth hinder your receiving the purifying baptism? 'Now is the accepted time.' Tell God that all the doubtful things shall be given up, and then go down before him, singing while you kneel:

> *Faith, mighty faith, the promise sees,*
> *And looks to that alone,*
> *Laughs at impossibilities,*
> *And cries, 'It now is done.'*

Yours affectionately,
WILLIAM BOOTH

Four
Purity Described

'Now the God of peace, that brought again from the dead our Lord Jesus ... through the blood of the everlasting covenant, make you perfect in every good work to do his will, working in you that which is well-pleasing in his sight, through Jesus Christ; to whom be glory for ever and ever' (Hebrews 13:20, 21).

My Dear Comrades,

Has anything I have said set anyone among you longing after the possession of the precious, the inestimable, blessing of a pure heart? Has anyone in your corps been heard singing:

> *O when shall my soul find her rest,*
> *My strugglings and wrestlings be o'er?*
> *My heart, by my Saviour possessed,*
> *Be fearing and sinning no more?*

It is those who 'hunger and thirst after righteousness' that are to be 'filled'. If this desire has been created, in any degree, I am delighted. Let me try and increase that longing, by holding up before your eyes some of the advantages that flow out of the possession of the blessing. And the first thing I mention that seems calculated to create this desire is the fact that:

1. A pure heart will ensure a holy life. But here does anyone who has not heard my previous explanation of this subject ask, 'What do I mean by a holy life?' I answer that it is a life that meets the requirements, and ensures the fulfilment of the promises of this holy book; a life fashioned after the life of the Lord Jesus Christ. It will, at the best, be very imperfect, have many weaknesses about it, and be subjected to many mistakes; but still, according to the light possessed, it will be a holy life.

Is not such a life desirable, my comrades? Is not a man who is able to live out his religion before his family, before his workmates, and before the world, highly privileged? Will he not be a means of blessing to those around him, whichever way he turns? Look at him.

He is honest and faithful in all his worldly dealings, in his shop, factory, home, or wherever he may come. He has an honest heart.

He is true to his promises and engagements. His word is his bond. You can trust him either in or out of sight. He has a true heart.

He is industrious. He neither shirks his duty, nor wastes his time, nor scamps his work. He has an industrious heart.

He is kind. He is loving to his wife, tender to his children, faithful to his comrades, considerate for his servants, gentle to the weak, sympathetic to the sick. He has a kind heart.

He is compassionate. He pities the poor, yearns over the backslider, fights for the salvation of sinners in public, and cries to God for their deliverance in private. He has a soul-loving heart.

He is a holy man. His secret life is holy. In thought and feeling, conversation and disposition, he is able to please God and do his blessed will. He has a pure heart.

Is not such a heart desirable, my comrades? I thank God for as many of you as have been brought, by divine grace, into the possession of this beautiful treasure, but I want you all to come up to this standard. I want you all to enter this holy state.

2. But, further, a pure heart will give you peace. It is a condition for peace. You cannot have peace without it. I am always saying to you, in one form or another, that you must not expect a life of uninterrupted gladness in this world. It cannot be. Our imperfect bodies, with all their pains and weaknesses; the temptations of the devil, and the miseries of a world in rebellion against God, prevent anything like a life of unmixed rejoicing for you and me.

But peace, 'the peace of God, the peace that passeth all understanding', is your birthright and, with a pure heart, the treasure shall be yours. I say again, that while you are here you must have certain strife. You cannot help it. You will have strife with the devil. War to the knife with hell. You will have strife with wicked men. They will fight you because you are for righteousness and God, and for the deliverance of men.

But, Hallelujah! In the heart that is purified by the Holy Spirit, and sprinkled with the Blood of the Lamb, the strife with God has ceased, the war with conscience is ended, the fear of death and hell is over. The soul possessed of a pure heart has entered 'the rest that remaineth to the people of God'.

Do you enjoy this rest, my comrades? Is the inward strife over? Oh, make haste and let the blessed Spirit, who waits to sanctify you wholly, cast out the enemies of your soul!

It is not your poverties, nor your persecutions, nor your afflictions, nor your ignorance, nor ever so many other things all put together, that prevent your perfect peace. Sin is the enemy; and when malice and indolence, and ambition and unbelief and every other evil thing has been cast out, your 'peace shall flow as a river, and your righteousness shall abound as the waves of the sea'.

3. Purity of heart is the condition on which God will enter and dwell in your soul. Now listen, my comrades, and cry to God for an increase of faith, seeing that what I am going to say is a great mystery. But it is, nevertheless, gloriously true.

God wants to live with you, not only in your home, but in your very heart. Poor and ignorant as you may be among men, and little noticed, nay, even despised, by the great and rich people of the world, yet God – the great God, whom the 'heaven of heavens cannot contain' – wants to come and live in your heart, and that not as a visitor only, but as an abiding guest.

An old writer curiously says, 'God is like the rich people in one respect. He has two houses, a town house and a country house. His town house is in the Celestial City, but his country house is in the hearts of his people.' Hear what he says himself: 'For thus saith the high and lofty One that inhabiteth eternity, whose name is Holy; I dwell in the high and holy place' and 'with him also that is of a contrite and humble spirit' in order 'to revive the spirit of the humble, and to revive the heart of the contrite ones'. Brother, sister, can you not hear him saying, 'Behold, I stand at the door and knock: if any man hear my voice, and open the door, I will come in to him'?

> *O joyful sound of gospel grace!*
> *Christ shall in me appear;*
> *I, even I, shall see his face;*
> *I shall be holy here.*

> *This heart shall be his constant home;*
> *I hear his Spirit cry;*
> *'Surely,' he saith, 'I quickly come';*
> *He saith who cannot lie.*

Will you not say, 'Amen, come in, Lord Jesus, and come quickly'? Will you not let all go that would prevent him entering? Will you not fling the gates of your soul wide open, and let him come in? If you will, go down before him just now and bid him welcome.

I have much more to say to you on this precious subject, but it must wait till another time. Meanwhile, wait no longer for a full salvation.

Yours affectionately,
WILLIAM BOOTH

Jesus, my All-in-all thou art,
My rest in toil, my ease in pain,
The medicine of my broken heart,
In war my peace, in loss my gain,
My life in death, my All-in-all.
In want my plentiful supply,
In weakness my almighty power,
In bonds my perfect liberty,
My light in Satan's darkest hour,
In grief my joy unspeakable,
My life in death, my Heaven in hell.

Five

Purity and Love

'But now being made free from sin, and become servants to God, ye have your fruit unto holiness, and the end everlasting life' (Romans 6:22).

My Dear Comrades,

Since writing my last letter, I have been visiting the Salvationists of Switzerland, Italy and France. Everywhere I find vast openings for The Salvation Army. Everywhere I have met with dear comrades longing to make the most of their opportunities; and everywhere, it has seemed to me, that more red-hot religion would make these comrades equal to the splendid chances of usefulness that lie right before them.

But is it not the same in Great Britain, America, Australia and in every other part of the world to which these letters will come? Is it not so in your corps? – Nay, is it not so with every individual soldier who reads these words?

Now, as I have explained to you before, by red-hot religion I mean hearts made hot with love for God, for comrades, for perishing souls, for noble work, and for every other good thing possible to men and women on earth or in Heaven.

I mean hearts made hot with holy love, such love as will compel us to toil and sacrifice for the welfare of the object cared for. Such love as will make its possessor the servant of those beloved, and exercise a self-denying mastery over the heart that experiences it. Such love will be like our Master's. For 'herein is love, not that we loved God, but that he loved us'.

Look at the mother's love. Does it not make her sacrifice time, comfort and health for her child?

Look at the patriot's love. Does it not compel him to turn his back on home, family, business, to fight and die for his country?

And so hot love in the Salvationist will make him lay health, time, goods, and all he possesses at the feet of his Lord, and there use all in blessing and saving the souls of men.

Now it is this spirit of love which makes this blessed heat in the souls of men and women. As the devil lights and feeds the fires of malice, ambition, selfishness, pride, lust, and the other evils that encourage and strengthen souls in their warfare with God, and carries them down the broad way to destruction, so the fierce heat of pure love, created and maintained by the Holy Spirit, makes the Salvationist watch and pray, toil and talk and suffer, careless of what it costs him in doing so, if he can thereby gain the blessed object on which his heart is set.

But the Holy Spirit only dwells, in all his mastering power and burning zeal, in souls that have been cleansed from evil; so that if you are resolved to spend your life in blessing and saving men, and fighting for your Lord, you must have a pure heart.

A pure heart will make you a blessing to those around you, and that not merely as a result of what you do, but from the fact of what you are. People will, no doubt, be drawn to love Christ, and seek salvation, and fight for the Army by what you say and sing. Your appeals and your prayers will all affect them; but if, in addition, you possess this treasure, they will also be led to God and holiness and Heaven by what they see you are.

A pure heart, as we have seen, makes a good life. Goodness is attractive; men respect it, and are drawn to it, for what it is in itself. Even if they are themselves the slaves of what is bad and devilish, they cannot help admiring what is holy and divine. And if this is the case with the slaves of sin and vice, it will be a thousand times more so with those around you who have already been captivated by the charms of holiness. To such hearts, your life, if governed and inspired by pure love, will be a constant source of light, and strength, and consolation.

This is what we call influence. It is something that is always going on. It is like the fragrance of a rose. You take the flower and place it in the middle of a room, and day and night it will send forth a sweet smell to all around. You have not to do anything to it, or with it. You need not wave it about, or pass it from one to another. It will spread abroad its pleasant perfume quite apart from any movement.

So it is with the soldier who enjoys purity of heart, and lives in harmony with the experience. A holy influence will be going out from him all the time, not only from what he says and does, but from what he is himself.

You feel the power, and the sweetness, and the genuineness of his spirit and devotion. And when you hear his testimony, or listen to his prayers, or hear his pleading with sinners, you feel this blessed influence proceeding from him wherever you find him.

As you look into his eyes, and shake his hand, or sit by his side, it will be there. When you see him in the furnace of affliction, or stand by his dying bed, or follow him to the grave; nay, long after he has passed from mortal sight, this influence will continue to flow out to you. For years to come, a sight of his photograph or the bare mention of his name will warm your heart, strengthen your courage, sustain your faith, and increase your love for all that is Christlike and true. Why is this, my comrades? It is because you believed he was a holy man. You admired his self-sacrificing life. You felt that he had a pure heart.

There is another inducement which should lead you to seek a pure heart, and that is because it will bring you into the possession of a good hope. This is a precious treasure. To feel that whatever clouds may darken the sky, or whatever sorrows may sweep over your soul, there is good ground for anticipating peace, and joy and victory in the future, must be a precious and desirable thing.

A soldier who knows that he sincerely loves God, and that he is living in obedience to him, has an inward assurance that God will care for him, whatever troubles may arise. Whereas one who feels that he has malice, hatred, pride, love of the world, and other wrongs hidden away in his secret soul, and who knows that he is daily neglecting his duty to his family or to himself, to his corps, or the poor sinners around him, can no more have a bright hope that God is going to make him a happy future than the sinners can expect that they are going to have Heaven at the end of a sinful life. He may hope for it, but it will be like the hope of the hypocrite, certain to be destroyed.

But when the soul has the witness of the Spirit and of a consistent life, to the possession of inward purity, it can look forward with confidence to victory over every foe, deliverance out of every sorrow and, in the end, glory and honour, immortality and eternal life.

Have these blessed experiences any charm for you, my comrades? Let me review them. I think they are entrancing.

There is the holy life that will always be the outcome of a holy heart. If the fountain spring is pure, the flowing waters of daily life and action will be pure also.

There is the peace of God that passeth all understanding, which is ever associated with inward holiness. 'The wicked are like the troubled sea, when it cannot rest, whose waters cast up mire and dirt.' Any evil left in the soul must make trouble. Purity and peace are bound together by God himself.

There is the presence and the indwelling of God as a flame of holy love, which is the strength and spirit of holiness. This is the fiery baptism which burns up hatred, and grudges, and self-seeking, and self-will, and purifies all our motives and affections.

There is the useful life and the holy example that flow from a pure heart, which will not only speak in favour of God and holiness while you live, but shall go on influencing the world long after you have passed to your reward in the skies.

There is a blooming hope of the future and the brightness of your crown in eternity. The realisation of all this glorious experience, my comrades, hangs on your possession of a pure heart.

These are only some of the inestimable blessings that flow out of this eternal spring of purity and power. Have you got this treasure? If so, Hallelujah! If not, I want you to go down and seek it now.

Yours affectionately,
WILLIAM BOOTH

SIX

Purity – Is it Possible for Me to Obtain this Treasure?

My Dear Comrades,

I can very well imagine that some of my soldiers, after reading what I have been saying about a pure heart, will be asking the question: 'Is it possible for me to obtain this treasure?'

I am aware that many people outside our borders openly assert that such an experience is impossible. They declare that no man or woman can live in this world without committing sin. They say that no matter how we hate our sins, or weep over them, or pray to be delivered from them, or trust in Jesus Christ for victory over them, we must be beaten in the strife and go on sinning or, at the best, keep on sinning and repenting, right down to the River of Death.

Now, with regard to this objection, I maintain with the Apostle John that not only is God willing and able to forgive us our sins – which no one who believes the Bible will deny – but that he is equally willing and able to cleanse us from all unrighteousness.

But before we go further, let us have another word of explanation. We must understand one another. What is it that I am saying? I reply, I am declaring to you who hear these words nothing less than the scriptural doctrine that God can keep you from committing sin.

Perhaps some of you will ask, what is sin? I reply that the same apostle, that is John, answers that question in such a simple manner that anyone can understand him. He says in his epistle that 'all unrighteousness is sin'. That is, whatsoever thing a man does, or consents to being done, in his thoughts, desires or actions, which he knows to be wrong, that is sin.

Now I affirm, on the authority of the Bible, that Jesus Christ your Saviour is able and willing to keep you from doing wrong. His name was called Jesus, that is, Saviour, because he 'should save his people from their sins'.

As I have shown you already in these letters, you may make mistakes; you may have temptations; you may be low-spirited; you may have pain in your body, perplexity in your mind, and anguish in your heart; the world may be against you; dark clouds may hang low, and the future be threatening; nay, you may, like Jesus Christ on the Cross, even feel as though God and man has forsaken you, and yet, in spite of all this and all else of the same kind, you can be kept from sin. In the name of my dear Lord, I assert that it is possible for you to have and to keep a pure heart.

Many of you believe this already – and are as sure of it as I am myself. But some may be in doubt. Let me try and make it plain to them.

First, you cannot doubt God's ABILITY to make and keep you free from sin. He who made you, and sustains you in being, who redeemed you on the Cross, who pardoned your sins, and wrote your name in Heaven, can surely do this for you. He who will raise you from the dead, and land you at last safely in Heaven, is surely able to keep you from breaking his commandments and grieving his Holy Spirit all the rest of the short time you may have to spend in this world! I am sure he can.

It will be a difficult task, perhaps, fixed as you are with your particular trials of body and soul, or circumstances. There may be something in your family or your business very strongly opposed to your leading a holy life. You may have tried before, again and again, but only to fail. You may be full of doubts and fears, even to despair, and nothing short of a great salvation will meet your case. But God will be equal to the undertaking. I am sure he will.

He has saved you from many sins already. Evil habits and passions, that used to reign over you, have been mastered; nay, some of them have been destroyed. Why, then, should not your prayer be answered?

Finish, then, thy new creation,
Pure and spotless let me be;

Let me see thy great salvation,
Perfectly restored in thee.

I see no reason why he should not do this. He is able to keep the angels from sinning. They do not keep themselves. It is his almighty arm that holds them up and prevents them from falling.

He will well be able to keep you from sinning when you reach the Celestial Land; and, thank God, he can keep you here. You believe he is mighty to save. You sing, and sing, and sing again:

> *All things are possible to him*
> *That can in Jesus' name believe;*
> *Lord, I no more thy truth blaspheme,*
> *Thy truth I lovingly receive;*
> *I can, I do believe in thee,*
> *All things are possible to me.*

Then, my comrades, if God is able to make and keep you pure, you cannot question his WILLINGNESS to do it. This must be equally plain to you, and yet it will bear looking at. It is very important indeed, that you should see – yes, and feel as well – that Jesus Christ is not only able, but perfectly willing – nay, waiting, even while this is being read to you – to take away from your hearts the evil things that have been the plague of your lives, for ever to keep them from coming back to harass, and wound, and torment you again.

The very nature of God proves his willingness to make you holy. All beings everywhere act out their nature. You see illustrations of this around you every day – wicked people delight in the wickedness of their neighbours. Good people find pleasure in their goodness. God is holy. He tells us so, again and again; and being holy and hating iniquity, he must abhor wickedness in men and women, and find the great delight of his heart in making them pure and good like himself.

I am sure that nothing would gratify him more, my comrades, than to take everything that is unclean out of your hearts and lives. Will you let him do it?

God tells us, in plain language, in the Bible, that he wants to make you holy. Listen to some of his words: 'Put on the new man,' he says, 'which after God is created in righteousness and true holiness. ... Be ye therefore perfect, even as your Father which is in Heaven is perfect. ... For God hath not called us unto uncleanness, but unto holiness. ... This is the will of God, even your sanctification.'

Jesus Christ came into the world, and lived and suffered and died that you might be made holy. This was the main object of his life and death and resurrection. 'For this purpose the Son of God was manifested, that he might destroy the works of the devil.' Paul says that 'Jesus gave himself for his church' – that is, for you and for me – 'that he might sanctify and cleanse us, and that he might present us to himself ... not having spot, or wrinkle, or any such thing; but that we should be holy, and without blemish.'

His love for his children proves his willingness to save them from their sins. No miser ever loved his gold, no patriot ever loved his county, no mother ever loved her babe, no father ever loved his boy; no, not all the love of all the created beings on this earth put together would equal the love which God bears to you, his children, my dear comrades. And knowing as he does, that sin is your great curse, he must, nay, he does, long to deliver you from it.

God has promised you a clean heart, if you will seek it. 'Wherefore come out from among them, and be ye separate, saith the Lord, and touch not the unclean thing; and I will receive you, and will be a Father unto you, and ye shall be my sons and daughters, saith the Lord Almighty.'

But I am also sure that God is willing to give you a clean heart, because he has done the work for so many of his servants in the days gone by, and for so many of your comrades in our present time. He is no respecter of persons. You are as welcome to wash away your inward iniquities, in the fountain opened for sin and uncleanness, as any other son or daughter of Adam. Oh, he will be delighted for you to step into the blessed stream at once!

If you are a holy man or woman you will help forward the war, and spread the glory of Christ's Name far more effectively than you will if you are not fully saved. Holy people are the great need of the world. I am sure they are one of the great wants of the Army.

Do you not feel in your heart, while I am talking to you, that the Holy Spirit wants you to be pure, and is waiting now to give you the blessing? The fire of desire for your sanctification is burning strongly in my heart while I write this letter. Does not your desire also rise up for this? I believe it does. Well, wait no longer! All things are now ready! Is not a holy yearning springing up within you? Go down this moment before God, and sing:

> *Will you, will you now enter in?*
> *Will you, will you wash and be clean?*

> *Oh, that the Fire from Heaven might fall,*
> *And all my sins consume!*
> *Come, Holy Ghost, for thee I call,*
> *Spirit of Burning, come!*

> *Refining Fire, go through my heart,*
> *Illuminate my soul;*
> *Scatter thy life through every part,*
> *And sanctify the whole.*

Yours affectionately,
WILLIAM BOOTH

> *More hard than marble is my heart,*
> *And foul with sins of deepest stain;*
> *But thou the mighty Saviour art,*

Nor flowed thy cleansing Blood in vain;
Ah, soften melt this rock, and may
Thy Blood wash all these stains away!

O grant that nothing in my soul may dwell,
But thy pure love alone;
O may thy love possess me whole,
My joy, my treasure, and my crown!
Strange flames far from my heart remove;
My every act, word, thought, be love.

Seven

Purity – God's Gift

'But we have this treasure in earthen vessels, that the excellency of the power may be of God, and not of us' *(2 Corinthians 4:7).*

My Dear Comrades,

I now come to one of the most important parts of this very interesting subject. 'How can a pure heart be obtained?' I think I hear you say, 'It is good, very precious, very desirable; oh, how I wish the treasure was mine! But how can I get it?'

Now, here I think it will be profitable for us to have a look back over the road we have travelled together while considering this blessed experience. And first of all, you will remember that I tried to show you what holiness was. I begged you not to set it too high, as though it meant anything like continued rapture or an every-hour hallelujah feeling. Then, I cautioned you against setting it too low – that is, regarding it as being consistent with anything like the commission of actual sin. Then I showed you how valuable the blessing would be to you, because it meant peace and usefulness, and the continued smile of God. Then I went on to explain that it was a possible experience, maintaining that, no matter whether rich or poor, young or old, married or single, God could cleanse you from all filthiness of the flesh and of the spirit, and enable you to be perfect in holiness before him all the days of your life. I come now to answer what I hope is the cry of many hearts, 'How can I find the Pearl of Great Price?'

Now you ask – 'What must I do to be pure?' and in reply I say that there is certainly something to be done, and something that you will have to do yourselves. To understand what that something is, you must keep well before your minds the fact that there are two forces or powers that have to unite in the purification of the heart.

The first is the Divine – that is, God.

The second is the human – that is, man, which means yourself.

God and man are partners in the transaction. This is nothing new; it is the same in the affairs of your everyday life. You use the natural abilities God has given you to buy and sell, and plough and plant; and, as the result, God gives you food and raiment. This was the case when you were converted; you repented and believed, and God saved your soul. It will be the same when you are sanctified. The great work of cleansing your heart, and keeping it clean, will be performed by God himself; but there will be some conditions which you will have to fulfill on your part.

From first to last it is 'God that saves'. Fix your mind well on that truth. If ever you have a pure heart, it will come from God's own hand. When Jonah arrived definitely at the belief that salvation was of the Lord, and trusted him for it, his deliverance was nigh; for we read that immediately the Lord spake unto the fish, and it vomited him on to the dry land.

Only God can take out of your heart the bad temper, pride, malice, revenge, love of the world, and all the other evil things that have taken possession of it, and fill it with holy love and peace. To God you must look; to God you must go. This is the work of the Holy Ghost; he is the Purifying Fire; he is the Cleansing Flame; he only can sprinkle you with the water that purges the dross and takes away the sin; he only can make and keep you clean. What a blessing it is you have a God who is not only so mighty, but so willing to save!

> *Yourself you cannot save,*
> *Yourself you cannot keep;*
> *But strength in him, you surely have,*
> *Whose eyelids never sleep.*

But then, as I have said, there is something to be done on your side, and chief part of that something is the exercise of faith. The apostles, met in council at Jerusalem, affirmed that God purifies the heart by faith. That is to say, where the soul comes to God, and offers itself to him for the doing of all his sacred will, and believes that, for the sake of Jesus Christ, he does then and there cleanse it from all sin, that moment the Spirit answers to the faith, the work of purity is done, and the soul can sing:

> *He tells me when, and where, and how,*
> *Just at his footstool as I bow;*
> *The Blood of Jesus cleanses now,*
> *This moment I believe.*

You will see, then, that:

1. *This purification is not effected by any human power.* No priest or officer can by his own force cleanse your heart. We can help one another by our example, by our testimony, by our exhortations, by our advice. There is not a soldier here who, if he will yield himself up to God, and trust him for full deliverance, will not at once receive power to bless and save those around him as never before. But no comrade has the power to reach in to the heart of a comrade, and cleanse it from the evil it finds there; that is the work of Jesus Christ alone. He can touch you this very moment with his loving blood-stained hand, and say, 'I will, be thou clean,' and the work will be done. You will not get a pure heart from your fellow-creatures; if ever the treasure is yours, you will get it from God, and you will get it by faith.

2. *Purification will not be effected by any ceremonials, meetings, kneeling at the mercy seat, singing of songs, or the like, apart from the Spirit of God.* These forms and observances can wonderfully

help you. Oh, what a marvellous influence goes out from soul to soul when comrades kneel together, and join heart and hand to seek God's sanctifying grace! But such gatherings will be a curse, rather than a blessing, unless they carry you on to that simple faith in God himself which claims and receives the sanctifying power.

3. *Purification of the heart, my comrades, is not by knowledge.* It is true, you must know something about the treasure you seek. For instance, you must know what purity means; that it is possible to you, and that God will give it to you when you trust him for it. But you may know all this, and a thousand times more, and be no nearer its realisation, if that is all.

The Israelites knew that Canaan was just over Jordan. They were quite sure of it. They could see the hills and dales of the country they had sought so long; but they were not in possession of the land, and died without ever setting their weary feet in it.

What a number of my dear soldiers love to read, and hear, and talk, and sing about holiness! They are never tired of the subject. They know all about it, but stop short of the faith which alone can bring them into its enjoyment.

4. *The purification of the heart is not by repentance.* Some people are always mourning over the sins of their hearts and the inconsistencies of their lives. Oh, how they hate their coldness and pride, and worldliness and bad temper, and the

other evil things that still cling to their heart and make them trouble. Oh, how ashamed they are of the feebleness of their love for Christ, the littleness of their zeal for his Kingdom, and the lukewarmness of their concern for souls. They are constantly giving up their evil ways and promising to do better. But this repenting and renouncing does not help them, because they do not go on to that definite act of faith that brings deliverance from the evils over which they mourn.

5. *The purification of your hearts, my comrades, will not come by your personal consecration to the service of God, if you simply stop there.* What you want is, not only the readiness to do the will of God, but the power to do it.

This purification is, as the apostle says, 'by faith'. It is by faith that the soul presses on beyond desire and knowledge, and repentance and consecration, and says, 'The blessing is mine.' This is the last round in the salvation ladder. You may have to climb up by all, or only some of the steps I have named; but you must reach this step, or you cannot enter the temple of holiness. You say 'I desire,' 'I repent,' 'I consecrate.' Good, very good, excellent; but can you, will you, not take the last step and say, 'I believe that he purifies me now'?

Yours affectionately,
WILLIAM BOOTH

Answer that gracious end in me,
For which thy precious life was given,
Redeem from all iniquity,
Restore, and make me meet for Heaven;
Unless thou purge my every stain,
Thy suffering and my faith are vain.

Didst thou not in the flesh appear,
Sin to condemn, and man to save?
That perfect love might cast out fear?
That I thy mind in me might have?
In holiness show forth thy praise,
And serve thee all my spotless days?

Didst thou not die that I might live,
No longer to myself, but thee?
Might body, soul, and spirit give
To him who gave himself for me?
Come then, my Master, and my God,
Take the dear purchase of thy Blood.

Eight

Purifying Faith

'That Christ may dwell in your hearts by faith; that ye, being rooted and grounded in love, may be able to comprehend with all saints what is the breadth, and length, and depth, and height; and to know the love of Christ, which passeth knowledge, that ye might be filled with all the fullness of God' (Ephesians 3:17-19).

My Dear Comrades,

You will remember that when I closed my last letter, I was considering a very interesting part of our subject; namely, that particular act of faith which purifies the heart. I said something to you then on this question; but I must have another word, because I fancy that it is here that many of my dear people stumble and fail in seeking the blessing of purity. They come to the door of full deliverance from sin; they look inside the temple of holiness; they long to be there; but they hesitate to take the step which alone can carry them in.

They cannot, or do not, or will not exercise the faith that purifies, and so turn away and go back to the unsatisfactory state of sinning and repenting in which they lived so long. Now, I feel quite sure that this is often caused by ignorance or mistaken notions; and I would, therefore, very much like to explain a little further what that wonderful faith is by which the soul enters into the enjoyment of a full salvation.

I may have again to pass over some of the ground we have already travelled together. But that cannot be helped. I had better repeat myself a thousand times and be understood, than leave you in doubt as to my meaning.

1. I remark that *purifying faith is the faith that has some definite knowledge of the nature of the blessing desired, and the means by which it is attained.* That knowledge may be very imperfect, but it is enough to apprehend the nature of the purity sought for. This faith sees that purity is not merely a passing wave of feeling or a deliverance from temptation. It perceives that it is not a condition of uninterrupted happiness, but a state of holiness in which the servant of God ceases to grieve the Holy Spirit, obeys the call of duty, and loves him with all the power he possesses.

Purifying faith fixes its eye on the blessing, and says, 'I want a pure heart, I need it; it is the will of God that I should have it. Christ bought it for me when he died on the Cross. O God, let it be mine.'

Has your faith got as far as that, my comrades? Do you see what purity means? If so, that is a gratifying attainment. Hold it fast until God bestows the great treasure upon you.

2. *Purifying faith sets the soul longing after the possession of this treasure.* Looking at a thing which you consider valuable and possible will certainly awaken the desire for its possession. If I am informed of some site of land, or some piece of property, which I could see would be of great service to the Army, the more I think about it, the longer I look at it, the more strongly shall I desire its possession.

It is so with holiness, my comrades. If you believe it to be the precious thing it really is, you will consider it, keep it before your mind, turn it round and round, and the more you do so the more you will desire it. Does your faith compel your attention? Does it make you think 'O Lord, increase our faith'? If you will only keep on looking at it you will come to long after it with earnest desire.

3. *Purifying faith is the faith that leads the soul to choose the blessing.* It says, 'I'll have it if it is for me,' and sings:

> *Give me the faith that Jesus had,*
> *The faith that can great mountains move,*
> *That makes the mournful spirit glad,*
> *The saving faith that works by love;*
> *The faith for which the saints have striven,*
> *The faith that pulls the fire from Heaven.*

Purifying faith goes further than merely admiring and talking, and longing and praying: it elects to make the experience its own. It says, 'Now,

Lord, this great deliverance shall be mine. I choose it. If it is to be attained, I'll have it!'

We all know how the sinners around us pain our hearts by the way they trifle with salvation. They say, 'Oh, yes, it is good, and it's very kind of Jesus Christ to make it possible for us to be saved. We must have salvation. We must not be lost. But we won't seek it now.' Even so, I am afraid many soldiers trifle with holiness. They say, 'I ought to be holy; I wish I were holy. O Lord, make me holy – but not now.' But purifying faith chooses the blessing desired. It says, 'I'll begin to seek now with all my heart – and I'll seek until I find.'

4. *Purifying faith compels the surrender of everything that stands in the way of the possession of holiness.* It is willing to pay the price. Oh, how cheerfully people give up pleasant things in order to gain those which they believe to be still more desirable. So here, when men really do see and believe in the worth of purity, they will be ready to abandon everything which seems likely to hinder them obtaining it.

Oh, my comrades, have you got thus far? Does your faith duly value the treasure we are talking about? If not, it cannot be said to be purifying faith. If it does, it will cry out

> *Is there a thing beneath the sun*
> *That strives with thee my heart to share?*
> *Oh, tear it thence, and reign alone,*

The Lord of every motion there;
Then shall my heart from earth be free
When it has found repose in thee.

5. *Purifying faith leads the soul to the consecration of all it possesses to the service of its Saviour.*

Now, my dear comrades, has your faith got as far as this? I am afraid many come close up to this point, and then grow afraid. They shrink from the full consecration, and give up the holy strife. They will say, 'If I place myself in the hands of God, for him to do just as he likes with me, who can tell where he may send me, or what he may want me to do?'

For instance, I fancy some of my soldiers hang back from the fear that God should say to them: You will have to put on the uniform; or you will have to speak to your relatives about their souls; or you will have to plead with strangers; or you will have to be officers, or do something else from which their unsanctified hearts turn back; and so they go no further in the search for purity.

But purifying faith sees Jesus Christ to be the altogether lovely, his service to be infinitely desirable, and the privilege of joining with him in the work of saving and blessing men so honourable and desirable that the soul controlled by it leaps forward to lay itself at the Master's feet, willing to be used in any way he thinks best, and so gladly offers a consecration which knows no hesitation, has no reservation, the limits of which being only bounded by its ability.

6. *But purifying faith goes further than this: it realises that holiness has been bought by the sacrifice of Jesus Christ, and is promised in the unchanging word of God.* Do you see that this treasure of treasures is yours, my comrades, and that God, having provided and promised it, is now waiting and willing to give it you?

Faith hears God say, 'From all your filthiness, and from all your idols, will I cleanse you.'

Faith replies, 'True, Lord, and I am waiting and longing for it to be done. It shall be mine.'

Faith hears him say, 'I will take away the heart of stone – the hardness from your heart – and give you a heart of flesh – a tender heart,' and answers, 'Lord, I am sure you will. I trust you to do it now. The hour of my sanctification is at hand. The cleansing Spirit is coming to dwell within me. He will make and keep me clean.'

7. *But purifying faith goes further still:* it believes that it actually receives the purity which its seeks. It says not only 'God is willing and waiting to save,' but 'Jesus does sanctify me now.'

My comrades, I want to ask you the question, 'When shall this purity come into your hearts?' Do you say tomorrow? I answer, 'Perhaps it may be tomorrow. I do not know whether it may.' Do you say, 'When I am dying'? I answer, 'Perhaps it may be when you are dying, but I do not know whether it will be possible then.' Do you say now? I answer, 'YES, IT CAN BE NOW,' for 'Now is the accepted time, and now is THE day of salvation.'

Yours affectionately,
WILLIAM BOOTH

Nine

Witnesses

'But ye shall receive power, after that the Holy Ghost is come upon you: and ye shall be witnesses unto me both in Jerusalem, and in all Judea, and in Samaria, and unto the uttermost part of the earth' (Acts 1:8).

My Dear Comrades,

Have you grown tired of my subject? I hope not. From my youth until this very day the subject of holiness has always had an unspeakable charm for me. To pray and hear, and sing and believe, and testify to the power of the precious Blood to cleanse from sin, and fill with love, and keep from falling, has been among the most precious privileges of my life. The charm is as fresh to me today as ever. I trust you feel as I do.

A devout saint of old sang in words that always thrill my soul when I hear them:

> *I'll carve his passion in the bark;*
> *and every wounded tree*
> *Shall droop, and bear some sacred mark*
> *that Jesus died for me.*
> *And men shall wonder as they read,*

inscribed through all the grove,
How Heaven itself came down to bleed,
to win a mortal's love.

Is not that beautiful, my comrades? Ought not we Salvationists to be anxious to sound out, by our lips and lives, to the sons and daughters of men, at every opportunity the glorious fact that Jesus Christ died not only to save men and women from open and deliberate sin, but to purify unto himself 'a peculiar people,' inwardly as well as outwardly clean.

Has he wrought this deliverance for you, my comrades? Or are you deterred from seeking it by doubts as to his ability to effect this purification of the heart? Let me call a few witnesses who will testify to its realisation in their own experience. I am sure you will listen to what they have to say.

I will begin with the saints of the Bible. Hear them. To begin with we read that:

1. *Enoch walked with God 300 years.* God himself testifies that Enoch's ways were pleasing in his sight. What a blessed testimony. Who can question that Enoch had a pure heart?

2. *Noah was a good man, and perfect in his generation.* So far as he had the light he lived up to it. He condemned the world and became 'heir of the righteousness,' that is the holiness 'which is by faith'. He had a pure heart.

3. *The Lord himself testified that Job was a perfect and an upright man.* He was perfect in love, and

perfect in faith. He was able to look up even in the darkest hour, and say, 'Though he slay me, yet will I trust in him.' He loved God with all his heart, and his neighbour as himself. He had a pure heart.

4. *We have a most remarkable testimony to Abraham's faith and obedience.* God told him, as he tells you, to 'walk before him, and be perfect,' and we have the most striking evidence of Abraham's obedience to God in the offering up of his son Isaac. Who can doubt that he had a pure heart?

5. *Isaiah was a holy man.* We read that when the prophet acknowledged his uncleanness in the Temple, God's angel touched his lips with a live coal of fire from off the altar, and testified that his iniquity was taken away and his sin was purged. Whereupon Isaiah rose up and consecrated himself there and then to go out as the messenger of God. He had a pure heart.

6. *Zacharias and Elizabeth his wife, we are informed, were both righteous.* They walked in all the commandments of the Lord blameless. Being delivered out of the hand of their enemies, they served God without fear, in holiness and righteousness all the days of their lives.

7. *The Apostle John testified that he was made perfect in love.* 'God is love,' he says; 'he that dwelleth in love, dwelleth in God, and God in him. Herein is our love made perfect, that we may have boldness in the day of judgment; because as he is, so are we in this world.'

8. *Paul called his comrades to witness that his life was a holy life.* 'Ye are witnesses,' he says to the Thessalonians, 'how holy, justly, and unblameably we behaved ourselves among you.'

But let me call a few witnesses of modern times. I testify that they belong to the choicest spirits who have ever walked this earth. I start off with the saint, John Fletcher, a clergyman. He says:

'I will confess him to all the world, and I declare unto you in the presence of the Holy Trinity that I am dead indeed unto sin; Christ is my Prophet, Priest, and King, my indwelling Holiness, my All in All!'

Hear another witness:

'All at once, I felt that a hand, not feeble, but omnipotent, not in wrath, but in love, was laid upon my brow. It seemed to diffuse through me a holy, self-consuming energy. The depths of God's love swallowed me up. All its waves and billows rolled over me.'

Hear the testimony of one of the holiest and most useful men ever possessed by the British Church – a man whom I admire more than words can tell:

'My soul was all wonder, love, and praise. It is now 26 years ago; I have walked in this liberty ever since. Glory be to God! I have been kept by his power. By faith I stand.'

A host of other testimonies are before me. One more is all I can find room for. Hear him. He says:

'I was alone in the field one beautiful day in the early spring. The sky clear, the sun glorious, the happy birds, and all nature, quick and springing into life, were but the symbol of my heart's experience. It was a glorious day within and without. I can never forget that day. I shall never enjoy a happier day until I walk the fields of Paradise. "What is it that you want?" seemed to be asked of me.

'"I want victory over all sin," was my answer. "Have you not got it?" "Yes," I replied. "What else do you want?" I answered, "I want power to perform all the known will of God." "Do you not do this?" "Yes," I answered, "Glory to God!" "Well, then, have you not received the blessing you have asked for?" And never from that hour have I doubted for a moment the reality of that work.'

Comrades, I have convinced you that there is no fatal necessity laid on you to sin, either in word, or thought, or deed. I have declared to you the unchanging faithfulness and power of your redeeming God. And now, what will you do? Your Lord is waiting to bring you into the land of perfect purity, of perfect love. I have shown you how you can enter in. Again I beseech you to rise, and go up to possess the good land, in God's own way; that is, by faith. But, do it now, and if at first you do not succeed, do not give up the search; but persevere, and try, and try and try again.

Yours affectionately,
WILLIAM BOOTH

Ten

How to Keep Pure

'Blessed is the man that endureth temptation: for when he is tried, he shall receive the crown of life, which the Lord hath promised to them that love him' (James 1:12).

My Dear Comrades,

After trying to show you the desirability of this experience, and urging it upon your acceptance, I cannot help feeling that a few counsels bearing upon the best method of retaining the blessing of holiness after it has been gained may be useful.

Beyond question many do find this sacred treasure of a pure heart, and exult in the confidence and joy it brings, who after a short season lose it again. They enter the Holy Temple, and then for one reason or another desert it. They struggle with tears and prayers up on to the highway of holiness, and then turn aside on to some bypath or other, where they become the prey once more of the doubts and fears and sins of the olden time. This is a great pity. Those who act thus are the chief sufferers; but, alas! A great injury is also inflicted upon others by their unfaithfulness.

But the failure of those who obtain the grace to keep what they have received should be no discouragement to you who have entered upon this holy path, and no argument against your persevering in it.

What you have to do, my comrades, is to make up your minds, that having found the pearl of great price no enemy shall rob you of the treasure. To this end, my first counsel is:

1. *Seek till you obtain a settled conviction in your own heart that the work is done.* Be content with nothing less than the assurance that God has really and truly cleansed your soul from sin. Do not allow yourselves to rest in any pleasant feelings merely, or in any hope of a future revelation on the subject. Continue to wrestle, and pray, and believe, until you are satisfied that the work is accomplished.

But do you ask again, 'How can I tell whether God has cleansed my soul from sin?' I reply, 'How did you find out that God had forgiven your sins? How did you come to know that precious fact?' for, assuredly, a precious fact it was when you were saved. I suppose that since that gracious gift was yours, you have sung, a thousand times or more, the words

> *I never shall forget the day*
> *When Jesus washed my sins away.*

'How did you come to the personal assurance that you were saved?' I ask, and you reply that God spoke it to your heart. Well, the assurance of your sanctification will come in the same way. The Holy Spirit will produce a delightful persuasion in your soul that all the pride and malice, and envy and selfishness, have been taken away, and that God has filled you with peace and love.

This precious persuasion will, no doubt, come in different forms to different individuals. To some it will appear as the 'Rest of Faith,' to others as the 'Baptism of Fire,' to others as the 'Fullness of Love,' and to others as the enthronement of Christ come to reign in their souls – supreme over an inward Kingdom, which is righteousness, peace, and joy in the Holy Ghost.

But to all alike, when the work is real and complete there will be the conviction that the Blood cleanses and that the heart is pure. Be content with nothing less than this, and leave to God's good pleasure the giving or the withholding of more.

2. *Being satisfied that God has purified your heart, confess the fact.* You must do so, if you want to retain the blessing. Many of the holiest men and women the world has known have, under the influence of false modesty or diffidence or other motives, been hindered from avowing the wonderful things that God has done for them, and have thereby grieved the Holy Spirit and lost the blessing. Satan will tempt you to hide your light under a bushel after the same manner, but you must resist him, and boldly confess to all around you the Salvation God has given you.

Acknowledge it to yourselves. Say over and over again to your own heart:

> *Glory, glory, Jesus saves me;*
> *Glory, glory to the Lamb;*
> *Now the cleansing Blood has reached me,*
> *Glory, glory to the Lamb!*

Acknowledge it to your Saviour. Tell him that you trust him, and glorify him for what he has done for you.

Confess it to your comrades at every reasonable opportunity. Let it be known in your own family. It may not only greatly help you, for those nearest and dearest to you to know what God has done for you, but it may prove a great blessing to them.

Of course you will be careful not to exhibit anything like a boastful spirit, and to give all the glory to God for all that he has given you to enjoy, and I am sure you will not make any professions as though you condemned those comrades who have not been brought to see and possess this great salvation. Love will be in all your words as well as in your heart.

But you must confess the fact that God has cleansed your heart, and that, by his Spirit, he enables you to live day by day without grieving him. It may be, at times it will be, a cross. But you must take it up, and in doing so you will become a light and a power and a joy to your comrades and friends.

3. *To retain the blessing you must strive to live in the same spirit of submission, obedience, and consecration to God* as that which you entered into its enjoyment. Your everyday experience must be that which we often sing:

> *Here then to thee thy own I leave,*
> *Mould as thou wilt thy passive clay,*
> *But let me all thy stamp receive*
> *And let me all thy words obey,*
> *Serve with a single heart and eye,*
> *And to thy glory live and die.*

4. *To keep this experience you must continue in the same spirit of trust that first brought the blessing into your heart.* You did not receive the gift of purity by feelings or by knowledge or by works; no, nor by desire nor by prayer. *You believed and you were saved.* If you had said, 'I won't, or I can't believe that Jesus cleanses, unless I feel the work to be done in my heart,' you could not have rejoiced in its possession. You trusted and the work was done. You must go forward in that spirit. There will be hours when all will seem to be hard and dark and desolate. Those will be the hours when you will have to fight the fight of faith, and to cling to the beginning of your confidence, whether you feel pleasant or unpleasant, whether your heart seems hard or tender, that the Blood cleanses. *Hold it fast!*

5. *To keep a clean heart you must resist temptation.* You will have temptation, it will come from different

sources, but especially from the devil, in three particular directions –

(a) He will try to draw you aside into old habits, either doubtful in their nature or positively evil. He will know your weak points. Set a double watch there.

(b) He will suggest his own evil wishes and desires, and then seek to persuade you that they are from your own heart. He will say, 'How can you be sanctified and have such sinful thoughts as those?' Disown his foul productions. Tell him they are not yours. Tell him that you hate them. Tell him they belong to him.

(c) He will strive to make you think you have lost the blessing because you do not always feel as though you had it. But you are to live not by feeling but by faith.

6. *To keep a pure heart you must carefully continue the use of such means as God has appointed for your assistance.* Purity does not bring you into any state that renders the use of means for its maintenance and increase unnecessary.

7. *To keep the blessing –*

(a) You must pray; and I strongly urge you to pray at stated hours, and for given periods.

(b) You must read and study your Bible.

(c) Read such books and papers as are instructive and encouraging on the subject of holiness.

(d) Watch as well as pray. Be ever on your guard.

8. *Keep on fighting for souls.* Do not be led off into a selfish occupation with your own experience, or in

promoting the same experience in other comrades. I think it is right and proper that you should devote a portion of your time and energy to the duty of sanctifying yourselves and of spreading a full salvation among your comrades. But nothing can relieve you from the duty of fighting for the salvation of dying souls around you.

I have only space for one other word. It is one of deep importance. With all the emphasis I can command I would say to every reader of these letters, if from any cause whatever you should lose the assurance that the Blood of Jesus cleanses you; or if, more melancholy still, you should lose the blessing of purity, fly at once to your Saviour's feet, confess your wrongdoing, give yourself up again to the full service of your Lord, and once more plunge in the fountain opened for sin and uncleanness; and then, profiting by the sorrow and disappointment of your fall, start afresh to live the life of faith in a purifying Saviour.

Yours affectionately,
WILLIAM BOOTH

What though a thousand host engage
a thousand worlds my soul to shake,
I have a shield shall quell their rage
and drive the alien armies back:
Portrayed it bears a bleeding Lamb,
I dare believe in Jesus' name.

Me to retrieve from Satan's hands,
*   me from this evil world to free,*
To purge my sins and loose my bands,
*   and save from all iniquity,*
My Lord and God from Heaven he came;
*   I dare believe in Jesus' name.*